COMFORT FOR THE JOURNEY

One Woman's Experiences With Multiple Sclerosis

Jane Goebel

With Kari Dahlin

2007

Comfort for the Journey
Copyright 2007 by Library of Hope
All Rights Reserved.
ISBN: ISBN. 0-9768438-8-9
Published by Library of Hope
www.libraryofhope.org
Colorado Springs, Colorado
Cover Design by Gary Carlson
Impact for Life Ministries
1107 Garden of the God's Road
Colorado Springs, CO 80907
719-632-3880
www.comfortforthejourney.org
Printed in the United States

Dedicated to the Glory of God

Dedication

To my loving husband and best friend who has modeled
to me the sacrificial love of Jesus Christ.

To Kari Dahlin, my special friend for, helping me write
this book. Your support has been invaluable!

To my family who continues to stand by my side with
their love and support.

To the countless people who suffer daily with chronic
conditions both physically and emotionally.

You are my Heroes!

Forward

It is with great pleasure and humility that I have been involved in this project with my dear friend Jane. When I first started to visit Jane a number of years ago, my purpose was to encourage and support her through the trials of living with multiple sclerosis. However, as often happens in these situations, I went to minister to her and soon found myself being the recipient of her ministry!

Jane's faith has been a tremendous witness to me. If you were to meet Jane, you would immediately sense her deep and abiding relationship with the Lord Jesus Christ. Her understanding of who God is and how He loves her is what has kept her going over the past thirty plus years since her first symptoms appeared. The God she worships is sovereign, greater than all other gods. He has absolute power and ultimate control over all that exists. Nothing happens to her that He doesn't already know about. Nothing can separate her from His love. He knows her future. He has a plan for her life and promises to give her all that is needed to fulfill that plan. He has already prepared a place for her in heaven where, some day, He will bring her home for eternity. Jane has learned these truths from God's Word, the Holy Bible. The best part is that they apply not only to her, but also to you!

Jane began the writing of this book several years ago when she still had strength and mobility to write and type. Her desire was to share with others what God was teaching her through her illness. She wanted to pass on the hope, comfort and encouragement she was receiving from the Lord.

Jane's efforts were hindered when she lost the use of both hands and could no longer transcribe her ideas from heart and mind to paper. She tried working with a few professional writers who were willing to volunteer their time and expertise but scheduling conflicts or communication difficulties stymied their efforts. It began to seem as if the completion of Jane's book would never happen.

Fully aware of all the struggles Jane was experiencing in completing this project, I wondered if I could be of any use to Jane. I had no professional expertise to offer, but I had time. Praying for God's anointing, I offered to be Jane's scribe and editor-of-sorts. Once again, I followed God's leading to serve and found myself being served as I learned essential spiritual lessons about submission and servanthood. My prayer has been that, as Jane submitted herself to the Lord to share His message through her, I would be able to submit myself, foregoing my personal style and opinions, to write Jane's words and heart.

What you now hold in your hands is a compilation of stories, Bible verses, special quotes, words of songs, and prayers from Jane's experiences. It is our prayer that this book will make its way to people who are in need of comfort and encouragement. Whether you are someone who has been diagnosed with MS or some other illness, are recovering from a life-altering accident or stroke, or are a caregiver, family member, or friend of someone who is suffering, we pray that you would find help in these pages. We don't know what you believe about who God is and what He has to do with you. Still, we pray Jane's words will stir in you a desire to know the only One who can truly soothe you, the Lord Jesus Christ. May you find His truth, love, blessing and peace to comfort you on your journey.

– Kari Dahlin

Introduction

When did you first learn that you, or someone you love, had a serious, debilitating illness? Do you remember where you were, what you were doing? Had you suspected the possibility as you privately made note of unusual symptoms, or as you met with doctors to find out what was wrong? What were your thoughts? What emotions do you recall feeling? Were you relieved to finally have a name to put to the physical changes going on? Were you afraid of what this would mean in your life? Were you unsure of what the diagnosis really meant? Were you too tired to care? One thing I have learned is that the journey through my disease, multiple sclerosis, is as varied in description as the number of people who travel it. No two passages are quite the same. The course of the disease is unpredictable. For some, the deterioration of the body happens quickly. For others, a fairly 'normal' life is led with periodic interruptions of more debilitating illness. A saying I've heard in the MS community goes, "The only consistency with MS is its inconsistency."

In COMFORT FOR THE JOURNEY, I address various topics drawn from my personal experiences of living with MS. Maybe my struggles will sound familiar to your own. I want to encourage you in some way, to bring comfort to you on your journey by sharing with you what I am learning. Please don't think, because I am writing about it, I have somehow conquered a particular issue and now have all the answers! In fact, I don't know if I will ever "arrive" at the place where I am able to live with MS unaffected by ongoing changes. But, I have hope in the midst of this journey. It is a hope that brings comfort and encouragement to me. I have written this book for one purpose – that you might also discover this hope, that you might also be encouraged as you travel this difficult road.

Contents

Forward

Introduction

Chapter 1   Comfort in Receiving My Diagnosis ……...................................1

Chapter 2   Comfort in the Midst of Physical Losses ……........................5

Chapter 3   Comfort in Taking Time to Rest …………..............................10

Chapter 4   Comfort When Worried …………….......................................14

Chapter 5   Comfort in Letting Go of Busyness………….......................18

Chapter 6   Comfort in Letting Go of Perfectionism …………...............21

Chapter 7   Comfort in Learning to Rely on Others …………...............24

Chapter 8   Comfort in the Shepherd's Arms …………..........................28

Chapter 9   Comfort in Discouragement …………….............................33

Chapter 10   Comfort in the Midst of Depression ………….....................37

Chapter 11   Comfort in the Darkest Place: Despair …………...............41

Chapter 12   Comfort in a Changed Perspective …………......................45

Chapter 13   Comfort in Praise and Worship …………...........................49

Chapter 14   Comfort in Family and Friends …………............................53

Chapter 15   Comfort in Seeing the Unseen …………….........................58

Chapter 16   Comfort in the Truth ………………..........................…...63

Chapter 17   Comfort in Finding the Blessing ………………...............…...66

Chapter 18   Comfort in Knowing Who I Am ……………….................…...70

God Desires to Give You Comfort in the Journey...........................73

Jane's Song …………………………………………..................…...75

Jane's Favorite Psalm ……………………………………….…...78

Comforting Scriptures for the Journey……………….....................80

    Adversity …………………………………….....................…...80

    Assurance …………………………………….....................…...82

    Depression …………………………………….......................83

    Discouragement …………………………………….................84

    Faith …………………………………….....................…...86

    Fear …………………………………….....................…...88

    Guidance …………………………………….......................89

    Patience …………………………………….......................91

    Prayer …………………………………….......................93

    Stability …………………………………….......................95

    Strength …………………………………….......................97

    Weakness……………………………………..........................98

    Wisdom …………………………………….......................99

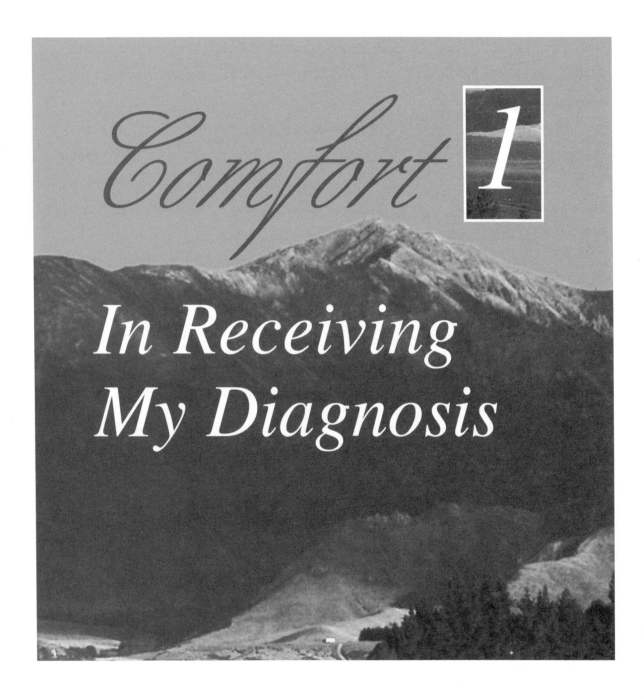

Comfort **1**

*In Receiving
My Diagnosis*

As Mel and I stood at the altar saying our wedding vows to be faithful in sickness and in health, little did we know how these words would be tested within eight years. On January 16, 1986, I was told I had multiple sclerosis. This illness is a chronic, unpredictable neurological disease impacting the central nervous system with a broad range of debilitating symptoms varying from one person to the next. For ten years prior to receiving this diagnosis, I had many and varying symptoms, but I never related them to just one cause. I reacted to the news with a typical grief response; I was in shock. Up to the point of my diagnosis, I was naive about how MS would impact my life. The finality of being diagnosed with an incurable disease caused me to wonder what the future would hold. I developed the habit of journaling my thoughts and feelings. On that first day I found it difficult to express with my own words what I was feeling, so my first journal entry was simply the lyrics of an old beloved hymn, "My Hope is Built on Nothing Less." Its words gave me assurance of God's dependability as I faced an uncertain future.

"My Hope Is Built on Nothing Less"
Text by Edward Mote (1797-1874) Public Domain

My hope is built on nothing less
Than Jesus' blood and righteousness;
No merit of my own I claim,
But wholly lean on Jesus' name.

Refrain: On Christ the solid rock I stand.
All other ground is sinking sand.

When darkness veils His lovely face
I rest on His unchanging grace.
In every high and stormy gale
My anchor holds within the veil.

His oath, His covenant, His blood
Support me in the whelming flood.
When all around my soul gives way,
He then is all my hope and stay.

When He shall come with trumpet sound,
O may I then in Him be found,
Dressed in His righteousness alone,
Faultless to stand before the throne.

As I look back on that day, I'm not surprised I struggled in my attempt to express myself. I wasn't in touch with my emotions. In spite of this, on that first evening of my diagnosis I was able to write in my journal in my own words, "I place my hope in God whose grace has supplied my every need in life. He's never left me nor forsaken me, and He promises He never will." This was the beginning of the multiple sclerosis journey I still travel. It's been a rough road with many twists and turns. Yet, God's grace has been and continues to comfort me. I believe His grace will do the same for you in facing life's challenges.

Jesus had perfect confidence in His Father, whose will He had come to accomplish.
Nothing touched Him without His Father's permission. Nothing touches me without
my Father's permission. Can I not then wait patiently?   He will show the way.

Elisabeth Elliot

~ Prayer ~

Dear LORD, I place my hope in You as I face an uncertain future. You alone are my
Rock and Salvation.

The LORD is my rock, my fortress and my
deliverer…in whom I take refuge. He is my shield.
Psalm 18:2

Even youths grow tired and weary, and young
men stumble and fall: but those who hope in the LORD
will renew their strength. They will soar on wings
like eagles; they will run and not grow weary,
they will walk and not be faint.
Isaiah 40:30-31

For the LORD comforts his people and will
have compassion on his afflicted ones.
Isaiah 49:13

4

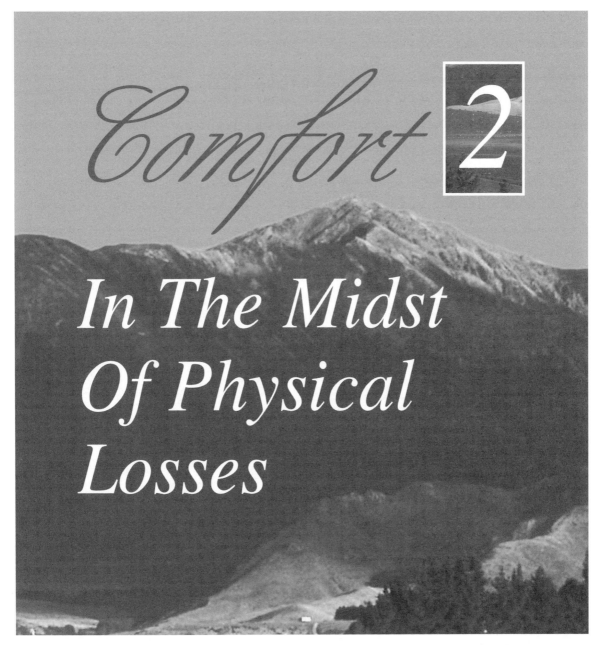

Comfort **2**

In The Midst
Of Physical
Losses

Multiple sclerosis is a disease that causes a steady drain of physical abilities and results in a perpetual cycle of grieving. For some, the rapid progression of your illness has caused you to suffer huge losses over a very short period of time. My heart goes out to you as you try to manage all the grief at once. Others, like me, have traveled a longer road with unpredictable bumps and turns along the way from your initial diagnosis to the place you are today. While this may appear to be an easier path because of the chance you have to adjust to each new symptom as it arises, having to continually be on the lookout for the next grief-inducing surprise is tiresome and anxiety-producing.

My personal journey began while I was a church organist. Numbness and tingling in my hands and feet threatened my ability to play the keys and pedals. As is common with this disease in the early stages, I would have bad days when the symptoms flared and good days when they would subside. I loved playing the organ and felt apprehensive about how these symptoms interfered. The flare-ups continued and became more frequent over time. I was enthusiastic about taking long walks and bike rides, enjoying the physical exercise and being outdoors. As the unexplained symptoms spread into my legs, weakening my muscles and causing my limbs to drag, I continued on until my body forced me to stop these enjoyable activities. I leaned heavily on my faith in God to give me strength to face what each day brought. Just as I did not know where this journey was taking me, I did not yet recognize the grief that followed me. I fought to deny or ignore what was happening to me, to continue on as if all was fine. But this attitude could not continue indefinitely.

I gradually lost control over my lower body. I was caught between the proverbial "rock and a hard place" as I struggled to accept the inevitable losses MS inflicted on my life. I fought giving in to the use of various appliances to keep me mobile as long as possible. First came a cane, followed by forearm crutches, a walk-er, an electric scooter and a power wheelchair ~ each represented a greater loss, a betrayal of sorts, as I admitted the reality that my body was prematurely failing me.

There were other particular losses to grieve that forced me to see MS for what it was, and loathe it for what it was taking from me. The ability to drive was one. I delayed that inevitable loss by learning to drive with hand controls. I had my van retrofitted with hand controls, which allowed me another year of independence. The last time I was able to drive was one early morning after dropping off my husband to pick up his car less than a mile away. Mine was the only vehicle on the road as I headed home. The trunk of my body had grown quite weak, making it difficult to hold myself up straight in the seat. Now it was slumping toward the center of the van and every effort to pull myself up again was futile. The fear I felt over the pos-sibility of having an accident was petrifying. No matter how resentful I felt about another loss in my life, I knew I had to come to terms with it.

It was also quite difficult and humbling for me to lose the capacity to care for my own basic needs. It was embarrassing to allow someone else to perform personal tasks of hygiene and grooming, such as showering and dressing me. When it became necessary to use a catheter, I was self-conscious and kept the bag hidden from view. Even with eating and drinking, I had to depend on someone else. I couldn't hold a pen, operate a keypad, scratch my own nose, or swat a fly from my face. It seemed MS was determined to regress me back to childhood, making me physically dependent and needy. I was still able to function with an adult mind and soul, though; I was determined to make my own decisions, handle my own affairs, and receive the same respect as any other healthy adult.

After living with MS for thirty-some years, I have come to understand that grief is a very natural emotion that encompasses a host of feelings. Grief unpacked includes denial, apprehension, fear, anger, guilt, blame, sadness, resignation and acceptance. These feelings occur haphazardly, in a random order that often includes backtracking. No two people grieve the same way or for the same length of time. No one can truly avoid grief, though we might try. Refusing to acknowledge and experience grief results in deeper emotional conflict as anger turns to bitterness, sorrow turns to depression, and disappointment turns to despair.

Even though I don't know you, I am absolutely certain that you, my friend, have grieved and will continue to grieve as you travel this journey. The comfort I have found has come by admitting my feelings to God. As I rely on His grace to help me identify my own feelings, He is faithful to help me accept the losses. God has my life in His hands. God knows my circumstances. He cares about how I feel. God is the One whose grace has supplied my every need in life so far. He is the One who has promised to never leave me or turn away from me. He is the One who has a plan for my future as He walks with me on this journey littered with losses. He is ready and willing to walk with you, too.

One morning as I prayed, I realized that because I could not see an answer, I was doubtful that there was an answer. My limitations became, in my mind, God's limitations. I had been praying as though my own needs might exhaust God's resources.

Elisabeth Elliot

~ Prayer ~
Dear Jesus, though my body is wasting away and I have suffered many physical losses, I thank you that none of them have gone unnoticed by You. You still have a plan for my life and you promise to be with me in the midst of my losses.

I will be glad and rejoice in your love, for
you saw my affliction and knew the anguish of my soul.
Psalm 31:7

I consider that our present sufferings are not worth comparing
with the glory that will be revealed in us. The creation waits in eager
expectation for the sons of God to be revealed.
Romans 8:18-19

Be joyful in hope, patient in affliction,
faithful in prayer.
Romans 12:12

Comfort 3

In Taking Time to Rest

Most MS patients are told over and over again that we have to learn how to pace ourselves. Because most of us have more energy in the morning, it makes sense to schedule appointments or errands then, and plan to rest in the afternoon. One woman in my support group would religiously schedule at least two hours a day when she would not be disturbed. She would not even answer the phone! Her discipline amazed me. It is hard for me to get into the habit of resting. Being a "doer," I think that I don't have time to rest. I already have too much to do with too little time! My reality is that it takes most of the morning just to get me ready for the day. I have to wait until the afternoon to schedule appointments. By late afternoon I feel tired, but I'm afraid that giving into a nap will keep me awake all night. I always find a reason not to rest.

In trying to convince me to allow myself a break more often, my doctor explained it this way. He said, "all people face each morning with a certain amount of energy to use. For people with MS, it is a limited amount. When it's used up, it's gone. Sand in an hourglass passes through the narrow center from the top bulb to the bottom to mark the passage of time. Once the top is empty, the sand is gone, and the hourglass is no longer useful. But, by turning over the hourglass, the sand begins to sift again and another hour is measured. For you, Jane, resting a bit each day is a little like turning over the hour glass. You won't be renewed as much as after a full night of sleep, but it is a way of gaining a little more energy to use."

It's not easy for me to allow myself a time to rest during the day. When I don't, however, I find that I am not only physically worn out, but I am mentally tired too, and I become easily overwhelmed with worry and anxious thoughts. When I do take time to quiet myself, I feel refreshed both physically and mentally. It calms my spirit and gives me enough energy to continue on with the day. I know a simple chorus that has helped me to quiet my thoughts and rest a few moments. Each verse is one sentence repeated over and over again. You might find repeating the words to yourself useful even if you don't know the tune.

Verse 1:   Be still and know that I am God. (Repeat three times)
Verse 2:   I am the Lord that healeth thee. (Repeat three times)

Jesus is in the boat with us, no matter how wild the storm is, and He is at peace. He commands us not to be afraid.

Elisabeth Elliot

~ Prayer ~
Gracious Father, I praise You that You are in control of all things concerning my life. You have given me the much-needed gift of rest for renewal of my mind, body and spirit. It is a gift You intend for me to use. Help me to take time for rest each day.

The LORD is good to those whose hope is in
him, to the one who seeks him; it is good to wait
quietly for the salvation of the LORD.
Lamentations 3:25-26

Be still and know that I am God.
Psalm 46:10

He got up and rebuked the wind
and said to the waves,
"Quiet! Be Still!"
Mark 4:39

Comfort 4

When Worried

There are times when troublesome thoughts fill my mind and heighten my anxiety. I worry about constant changes in my physical symptoms, whether a medication is working the way it should, whether I need more or less of it, or whether I would benefit from trying something different.

When I'm not sleeping well at night and can't turn on some music, read a book, or roll over on my own, it leaves me with too much quiet time to let my mind wander. I think about how tired I'll be tomorrow and how that will affect my emotional state. My limited ability to take action about my concerns or to have control over how others do things for me adds to my worries. Sometimes, the circular race-track seems never-ending.

At times like these, an old hymn comes to mind and gives me comfort.

"I Must Tell Jesus," Words by Elisha Albright Hoffman,
Public Domain

I must tell Jesus all of my trials;
I cannot bear these burdens alone;
In my distress He kindly will help me;
He ever loves and cares for His own.

Refrain
I must tell Jesus! I must tell Jesus!
I cannot bear my burdens alone;
I must tell Jesus! I must tell Jesus!
Jesus can help me, Jesus alone.

I must tell Jesus all of my troubles;
He is a kind, compassionate friend;
If I but ask Him, He will deliver,
Make of my troubles quickly an end.

Refrain
I must tell Jesus! I must tell Jesus!
I cannot bear my burdens alone;
I must tell Jesus! I must tell Jesus!
Jesus can help me, Jesus alone.

I cast all my cares upon you,
I lay all of my burdens down at your feet,
And any time I don't know what to do,
I will cast all my cares upon you.
And any time I don't know what to do,
I will cast all my cares upon you.

I have noticed how God intervenes when I am worried and anxious. He teaches me how to still my mind and find rest in Him. Isaiah 26:3 offers this promise, God will keep me in perfect peace because my mind is fixed on Him, and I trust in Him. I fix my mind on Him by recalling and meditating on scripture verses and songs I've learned in the past. When I turn my mind over to the Lord and focus on Him, my worries begin to fade. It is comforting to remember that I can trust God to take care of me in the midst of my worry. Jesus said, "Therefore I tell you, do not worry about your life, what you will eat or drink; or about your body, what you will wear. Is not life more important than food, and the body more important than clothes? Look at the birds of the air; they do not sow or reap or store away in barns, and yet your heavenly Father feeds them. Are you not much more valuable than they? Who of you by worrying can add a single hour to his life? (Matthew 6:25-27)

If it's time to work, get on with your job. If it's time to go to bed, go to sleep in peace. Let the Lord of the universe do the worrying.   Elisabeth Elliot

~ Prayer ~
Father, I thank you that you gently calm my mind and give me rest. Thank you for hearing my anxious thoughts and comforting me with your peace. May you be glorified.

Therefore do not worry about tomorrow,
for tomorrow will worry about itself.
Each day has enough trouble of its own.
Matthew 6:34

Do not be anxious about anything but
in everything, by prayer and petition, with thanksgiving,
present your requests to God.
Philippians 4:6

Cast all your anxiety on Him because
He cares for you.
I Peter 5:7

Comfort 5

_In Letting Go
of Busyness_

Living with MS has caused me to face limitations and let go of a busy lifestyle. Once, I had the stamina and drive to maintain two full-time positions at my church. One job, as the parish administrator, involved a traditional forty hours each week. The other job, as the church's organist, entailed weekend and occasional evening hours. But, as my energy level began to decline, it became increasingly difficult for me to meet the demands of both jobs. I hated to give up either job, or to admit I couldn't do it anymore. My work was my ministry, my way of serving God. When we moved to a new state, I regretfully decided to seek only one part-time position, hoping I would be able to manage at least that much. However, fatigue continued to rob me of my stamina until even my limited work schedule was too much. It was a very sad day for me, when I finally gave up working outside of our home altogether.

Letting go of busyness has been an ongoing challenge for me. I like having plenty to do, being able to control my own schedule. I derive a certain amount of comfort in having a predictable routine, knowing what to expect and what I can count on. Fatigue and loss of energy that commonly occur with MS have changed all that for me. Having a routine schedule is a dream of the past. I don't know at the beginning of each day how much energy and stamina I'll have throughout the day. Before, if I had had a poor night of sleep or felt tired during the day, I was typically able to push past the weariness. Now, if I feel tired, I truly am tired. Trying to ignore my need for a break makes it worse. It's like hitting a brick wall; there's no going past it until I give in and take a nap. I thank God for helping me adjust to a new routine.

Jesus knows we need time to slow down in our lives. He instructed His disciples to "Come away to a deserted place and rest awhile" (Mark 6:31). He also encouraged His friend and hostess, Martha, to leave her work in the kitchen, to sit with Him and to listen, as her sister Mary was doing (Luke 10:38-42). He reminds us to pause for rest in the midst of our busy schedules, to take a break and allow Him to refresh us. Giving myself permission to slow down has been difficult for me. As I release my plans and allow the Holy Spirit to schedule my time according to God's priorities, I find comfort and peace.

~ Prayer ~
Dear Jesus, thank You that You recognize my need for rest, for times of coming away from busy activities. Help me to be in tune with my energy level. Teach me to let go of my expectations and plans, and rest in you.

He who dwells in the shelter of the Most High
will rest in the shadow of the Almighty.
Psalm 91:1

Come unto Me, all you who are weary and
burdened, and I will give you rest.
Matthew 11:28

Be joyful in hope, patient in affliction,
faithful in prayer.
Romans 12:12

Comfort **6**

*In Letting
Go of
Perfectionism*

Perfectionism has impacted my life for years. I remember from an early age that everything I did needed to be "just right." I held an unrealistic expectation for myself. Often, I would put demands on my time and activities that prevented me from really enjoying life. The never ending "to do" list became a challenge for my perfectionism.

I think everyone to some degree is a perfectionist. We all have areas or things we do that we want to do with excellence. However, my perfectionism was obsessive compulsive.

Slowly, as my health continued to fail, I had to rely on others to do tasks for me. During this transition, it was difficult to accept the help of others. I had to learn that everyone completes tasks differently. Over time, I came to appreciate that it really didn't matter how the task was completed but that I had help to complete the task. I also learned to appreciate the qualities of people and their special gifts as they served me.

God has taught me to let go of my perfectionism and appreciate his servants who now complete all of my tasks. I am very grateful and comforted by their service to me.

~ Prayer ~
Gracious Father, thank You for helping me let go of my perfectionism to discover Your comfort through those who serve me.

The end of a matter is better than its beginning,
and patience is better than pride.
Ecclesiastes 7: 8

Be completely humble and gentle;
be patient bearing
with one another in love.
Ephesians 4:2

I can do everything through him
who gives me strength.
Philippians 4:13

Comfort **7**

In Learning to Rely on Others

Like most people, from the time I was a little child I wanted to do everything for myself. Being able to do things for myself meant I was growing up. I looked forward to becoming an adult and using my natural inclinations toward organization and efficiency to successfully manage my independence. Before I was diagnosed with MS, I enjoyed developing my own interests, going to college, traveling, finding a job in my chosen field, and keeping physically fit. I became a wife and liked keeping an orderly, clean home. When I was diagnosed with MS, the physical changes I experienced led to a gradual loss of independence that sometimes conflicted with my natural inclinations.

Losing independence has put me in the unwanted position of having to learn to accept help from others. The fact that it has been a necessary lesson has made it no less difficult. I recall the ambivalent emotions I felt when I first allowed someone to clean my home. It was a challenge to rely on someone else to do the tasks that I was used to doing myself. I no longer had control over the organization or efficiency of how things were done. Tasks were not carried out the way I would have done them. Feelings of frustration and irritation churned in me, as I tried to rely on others.

One day my pastor asked me how I was doing. Even though I wasn't proud of my feelings, I decided to be honest with him and voice my complaints. He sympathetically heard me out as I expected, but then he surprised me. "Jane," he said, "What difference does it make? What is going to happen if they do it that way?" I sheepishly admitted, "Nothing would happen."

I began to realize that my feelings were more about grieving my loss of control than how and when things were done. Becoming dependent on others has meant, at least to some extent, learning to submit my will and rely on others to help me. That's exactly what God asks us to do with Him. He knows that we don't naturally want to give up our control. He knows how I struggle with wanting to control and the need to do things my own way is the very essence of what He calls "sin". God is teaching me to rely on the help of others more graciously as I submit my will to Him. He is showing me how blessed I am by those who are willing to assist me with various tasks. I'm learning to let go of "my way" of getting the job done, to let go of the insignificant things of this life, and focus on loving those He sends my way. I am learning to rely on His strength to change a life-long pattern of trying to control my world. I take comfort in Jesus words, "My grace is sufficient for you. My power is made perfect in weakness." (2 Corinthians 12:9)

Withholding any part of ourselves from God is the same as saying, 'Thy will be done up to a point; mine from there on'.   Elisabeth Elliot

~ Prayer ~
Father, thank You that Your grace has been there to help me rely on others. Remind me that You are in control of my life. Help me to give up control.

Two are better than one, because they have a
good return for their work; if one falls down,
his friend can help him up.
Ecclesiastes 4:9-10

"I will not leave you as orphans;
I will come to you."
John 14:18

I can do everything through Him who
gives me strength.
Philippians 4:13

Comfort 8

In The Shepherd's Arms

One of the many lessons I am learning as I have become more dependent on others, has to do with patience in waiting. It is humbling for me to admit I am unable to do something for myself, and need to ask for help. Adding to my struggle, I find I am often at the mercy of someone else's time-table. It is hard for me to wait patiently for someone to complete my tasks, when I see so many things that could be done. Because I am a very efficient person by nature, I rarely allowed myself idle time. There was always something on  my "to do" list that I could fit in while I waited. With plenty of time on my hands now, I find my mind wandering, stewing, and entertaining negative, self-defeating thoughts.

For instance, I periodically need to change position in my chair to relieve the pressure on my spine, or to sit taller, or to face a different direction. Since I am unable to mobilize my body or my position, I must ask someone to help me and then wait until he or she is ready to do it. During the evenings when my husband is home with me, he is the one I turn to. He is always there to serve me. Sometimes, when he is occupied I have to wait. My bodily discomfort increases and feelings of irritation, resentment, and self-pity stand at the door of my heart waiting to inhabit me. My focus turns to negative thoughts about myself, about my plight, about my husband - an internal grumbling grows. My mind races from one thought to another as I try to combat bad feelings. I can quickly fall into the pit, thinking I'm not important or my husband has abandoned me. However, in reality He is always there for me and sees that I have adequate care. Yet, at times I experience feelings of loneliness and rejection knocking at my door. Once I've started down this slippery path it's very hard to stop. Rationally, I know these thoughts and feelings are not true, certainly not from God. Still, once they've gained a foothold, they aim for the very core of my being.

God warns us about the possibilities of becoming trapped by our negative thoughts and feelings. He tells us in the Bible to be on guard, watching out for them. He advises us to train our minds to focus on "whatever is true, whatever is noble, whatever is right, whatever is pure, whatever is lovely, whatever is admirable – if anything is excellent or praiseworthy, think about such things" (Philippians 4:8). Doing this takes practice and discipline. One exercise I have found helpful is to look at, or at least visualize in my mind's eye, a picture I have in my home (see the picture on the previous page). The central figure is of a strong and tender shepherd holding a small lamb in His arms. I train my mind on that image of Jesus and I imagine myself as that lamb in His arms. He is holding me tenderly and I am snuggled against His chest. I imagine how calming it is to hear and feel the beating of His heart. His arms embrace me securely, so that I feel safe and loved. I am reminded that He knows my name, that He created me for His own pleasure, and that He has made me His own by dying for me. It is comforting to know that He has given me His Holy Spirit to always be with me.

Does God seem absent? For most of us, He sometimes does. Even at such a time, may we not simply be still before Him?

Elisabeth Elliot

~ Prayer ~

Precious Jesus, thank you for being my comforting shepherd. You are the One that holds me close to your heart. Like a lamb in Your arms, I will depend on You.

The LORD is my shepherd,
I shall not be in want.
He makes me lie down in green pastures,
he leads me beside quiet waters,
he restores my soul.
He guides me in the paths of righteousness
for his name's sake.
Psalm 23:1-3

He tends his flock like a shepherd;
he gathers the lambs in his arms and
carries them close to his heart;
he gently leads those that have young.
Isaiah 40:11

"I am the good shepherd;
I know my sheep
and my sheep know me –
just as the Father knows me
and I know the Father –
and I lay down my life for the sheep."
John 10: 14-15

Comfort **9**

*In
Discouragement*

When I feel discouraged and unable to sleep at night because my mind runs wild with self-defeating thoughts, I remember a particular lullaby I've heard before. Although I'm not able to sit up and play the recording of it, I am comforted just recalling the soothing melody and lyrics. It's like a conversation between my Heavenly Father and me.

First, one voice starts expressing words that seem to come straight from the Father's heart. Without even having to express my complaint to the Lord, He seems to already know what is troubling me. He reminds me that I am safe because He is with me.

Then, a new voice sings the next lines, as if echoing my own thinking, especially when I am worn down from struggling with my condition. My voice confesses to God my own fears and distress. I imagine the Lord listening compassionately to my complaints. In patience, He allows me to express my sorrows and doesn't walk away from me, as I might expect a friend to do. Instead, He gently repeats His words of love, assuring me He knows exactly what I feel and offering me comfort beyond my understanding.

Finally, the voices mingle responsively, even as I wearily sink into His arms. He continues to comfort, as my complaints sound more like excuses for why I've been unable to rest, until at last I give in to Him. Just as a parent rocks a child to sleep with sweet lullabies sung softly, so my Lord holds me and whispers, "Rest, close your eyes; be at peace."

Here are the words of that lullaby:

Rest In Me (A Shepherd's Lullaby)
Written by Derri Daughert and Ellie Bannister; 2002 Banistuci Music

Verse 1:   (God sings to us)
Rest my child, you're safe right here. Close your
eyes. I see those tears. And I know how your heart
grows tired of life and its trials. Please lie down,
still your mind, quiet all your thoughts, and you will
find, even though you're an imperfect child, you're
still mine, and I love you.

Verse 2:   (We sing to God)
Lord, I'm just scared and I feel unprepared and
sometimes I just feel like I'm wandering around; And
the night feels so cold, and my sin grows so old, and
I do what I don't want to do. Help me hide where I
long to abide, in the shadow of your love.

Verse 3:   (God sings to us)
Hush my child, fall into my arms. I'll give you rest,
right where you are. Yes I know, you feel lost and
alone. Let me hold you; how I love you.

Chorus
God sings: **We echo:**
Rest my child,   Lord my heart is so tired

And trust in me   I'm a stumbling child

I'll give you life   Lord I'm so weak
and everlasting peace

Don't you know   And I fall at your feet
From long before time   Cover me with your wings

You have been mine   You are my
                                    prince of peace

Sung in unison: And I love you.

~ Prayer ~
Lord, how wonderful it is to realize that You know my feelings of discouragement.
Help me to remember how closely You hold me, because You love me.

Give ear to my words, O LORD; consider my sighing.
Listen to my cry for help, my King and my God, for to you I pray.
Psalm 5:1-2

"Though the mountains be shaken and hills be
removed, yet my unfailing love for you will not be
shaken, nor my covenant of peace be removed,"
says the LORD who has compassion on you.
Isaiah 54:10

We are hard pressed on every side, but not
crushed; perplexed, but not in despair; persecuted,
but not abandoned; struck down, but not destroyed.
2 Corinthians 4:8-9

Comfort

10

In The Midst of Depression

When I am feeling depressed, I can identify with the Psalms. The authors express their deepest feelings to God, laying their hearts open before Him with complete trust, daring to share and finding relief as they release their emotions to Him.

Psalm 13, which was written by David, asks many questions. "How long, O LORD? Will you forget me forever? How long will you hide your face from me? How long must I wrestle with my thoughts and every day have sorrow in my heart? When is this going to end?" I can identify with questions like these. What confuses me is how David ends his lament, "But I trust in your unfailing love, my heart rejoices in your salvation. I will sing to the Lord, for he has been good to me." He makes a sudden turn around from depression to praise! It's not that easy for me.

As I look back at the beginning of the Psalm, I notice that David honestly confessed his feelings of depression to God. Maybe his complete openness with God made it possible for God to change his heart. I want to deny my feelings because I think I "shouldn't" feel that way. Some people want to explain and justify their feelings, almost wearing them like badges to gain pity. Sometimes I feel like a victim of my feelings, and fear there is no way out of them. David's psalm shows me the importance of admitting where I'm at, so that God can take over and work in me His peace that brings comfort and praise.

Note too, in David's writings, how he often went from focusing on his negative feelings to focusing on the goodness of God. Giving praise to God, no matter how I feel, can help change my focus from me to Him. It's not that I should lie about the depression and try to hide it from the Father. After confessing my honest feelings, David's psalm seems to suggest that I should move on to praising God.

Some days, the depression feels so overwhelming that I can think of nothing else. It is good to remember that God is greater than my feelings. God's truth is more important than my emotions. If only out of sheer obedience, I can at least take comfort in saying these words out loud: "For I shall again praise You!" The truth is, I may not "feel" like praising God, but I will praise Him because He tells me to do it. Someday, my feelings will change, like a light being turned on, and I will be able to praise God again with ALL of my being.

God will not leave us alone. He goes through the valley, the deep water, the furnace. He will never, absolutely never, leave us or forsake us.

Elisabeth Elliot

~ Prayer ~
Father, I thank You that You hear my cry and comfort me in my depression. Help me to realize that You will never abandon me no matter how I feel. You are a wonderful God. All honor and glory are Yours.

I waited for the LORD; he turned to me and
heard my cry. He lifted me out of the slimy pit, out
of the mud and mire; he set my feet on a rock and gave
me a firm place to stand. He put a new song in my
mouth, a hymn of praise to our God.
Many will see and fear
and put their trust in the LORD.
Psalm 40:1-3

Why are you downcast, O my soul?
Why so disturbed within me?
Put your hope in God,
for I will yet praise him,
my Savior and my God.
My soul is downcast within me;
therefore I will remember you…
Psalm 42:5-6

He heals the broken hearted
and binds their wounds.
Psalm 147:3

Comfort **11**

In the
Darkest Place:
Despair

I have been to a terrifying place of deepest darkness. In it, I strain my eyes to see some context, some boundary or shape in the endless nothingness, but the darkness cannot be penetrated. It blinds me. I call out, but the sound is swallowed up in an airless vacuum. I struggle to communicate the vivid nightmare of thoughts that fill my mind, but my words mutate into garbled confusion. The shroud of death envelops and isolates me from reality. I am in the place of despair where hope is lost and depression reigns. In despair, I feel certain that even my Lord has deserted me. "Oh, that my end would come," my heart cries out in anguish. Not even an echo returns to me. I feel so utterly alone. Every day, my fear grows on the poisonous food of seductive lies: "You are alone, Jane. No one is able to understand or help you. There is no way of escape. Give up; give in. Despair is all there is." Although a part of me knows these thoughts are not true, I cannot seem to dispel them.

King David must have known the darkness of despair I have experienced. In Psalm 69 he wrote, "Save me, O God, for the waters have come up to my neck. I sink into the miry depths, where there is no foothold. I have come into the deep waters, the floods engulf me. I am worn out calling for help; my throat is parched. My eyes fail, looking for my God." (Psalm 69:1-3). Even Jesus, God's Son, knew the same desolation. When He died on the cross, He suffered the agony of complete separation from God, crying out, "My God, My God! Why have you forsaken me?" (Matthew 27:46). The comfort God gives is three-fold. First, He reminds me that I am not alone in the darkness of my despair. He is with me even when I cannot see Him or feel His presence. Second, He assures me that He knows from personal experience the depth of my suffering. Third, God instructs me to rely on His Holy

Spirit for guidance.

Romans 8:26 explains, "In the same way, the Spirit helps us in our weakness. We do not know what we ought to pray for, but the Spirit himself intercedes for us with groans that words cannot express." As I trust God to guide me out of despair, my panic is quieted; my heart is calmed; my mind remembers and clings to the Truth. Trusting Him is an act of faith, not dependent on my transient feelings or senses. In believing God is Who He says He is, I find peace in the darkness and patience to wait on Him to set me free.

I will never, never, never, never, never, (the Greek has five negatives) leave you or forsake you, is his promise. At times we may be overcome with a feeling of helpless forsakenness. Take God's own promise with its five negatives, and hold on.

Elisabeth Elliot

~ Prayer ~
Father, even when You seem so far from me, help me to believe Your Truth that You will never leave me nor forsake me. Thank You that Your love for me is not depend-ent on how I feel.

Then you will call, and the Lord will answer;
you will cry for help,
and he will say: "Here am I."
Isaiah 58:9

"Do not let your hearts be troubled.
Trust in God, trust also in me."
John 14:1

For I am convinced that neither death,
nor life ...nor anything else in all creation,
will be able to separate us
from the love of God in Christ Jesus
our LORD.
Romans 8:38-39

Comfort **12**

In a Changed
Perspective

In our fast-paced society, many people seem to have little tolerance for interruptions and delays in their hectic schedules. Instantaneous results are expected. Having to wait for someone or something is only a minor irritation for some, but becomes an excuse for "road rage" and other such emotional outbursts for others. "Waiting time" is "wasted time" that leads to lack of stimulation, boredom, and loss of productivity. Instead of giving in to frustration, when I used to find myself in a waiting situation, I tried to view it as an opportunity to practice patience. It helped to always have something with me to do. I didn't necessarily like waiting, but I tried to be productive with it anyway.

MS, as is typical, brought change for me in the world of waiting. The amount of time I spend waiting has increased dramatically. I have become more dependent on someone else to do simple tasks I used to do for myself. Now I must enlist the help of others and wait for them to respond, as they are available. Now I am at the stage where there's very little I can do on my own beyond thinking, talking, observing and listening.

A common waiting time for most people happens when they have a medical appointment. MS has not only added more appointments to my schedule, but it has also made it progressively more difficult to utilize the waiting time well. The way I used to cope by keeping busy with various tasks is no longer possible. Increased waiting time with decreased coping methods could be a recipe for disaster.

God has an interesting way of working in our lives. In this case, He chose to use MS to open my eyes to see some things I'd never taken time to see before, both literally and figuratively. He has been teaching me that waiting time can be a quiet, reflective time to notice the overlooked surprises, joys, and bits of encouragement, rather than a test of patience. I might gaze out my window and notice new wild flowers springing up in the prairie grass in the field behind my house. I might watch the constantly changing miraculous beauty of the sun setting behind the mountain ridge. My ears tune in to particular background sounds, catching words of a song playing on the radio that unexpectedly comfort and encourage me. Waiting time is a great time for praying, for praising God for love and beauty even in the small things, for observing people around me and offering a prayer for them even though I may know nothing of their situation. I know that God knows them, intimately and may be waiting for me to intercede on their behalf, asking Him to meet their needs. My perspective of time has changed with MS. I can't be in a hurry, but I don't have to complain or lose patience. Now I am finding a blessing in waiting with the new perspective God has given me. He is teaching me to be thankful and to pray.

God is not finished with us yet, whatever the loss we suffer, for as we loose our hold on visible things, the invisible become more precious – Where our treasure is, there will our hearts be.   Elisabeth Elliot

~ Prayer ~
Holy Spirit, Help me to see my times of waiting as opportunities to pray, to see evidences of You in my surroundings, and to make the best use of this time.

"For my thoughts are not your thoughts,
neither are your ways my ways,"
declares the LORD.
"As the heavens are higher than the earth,
so are my ways higher than your ways
and my thoughts than your thoughts."
Isaiah 55:8-9

Devote yourselves to prayer,
being watchful and thankful.
Colossians 4:2

Give thanks in all circumstances for this is
God's will for you in Christ Jesus.
I Thessalonians 5:18

Comfort

13

In Praise and Worship

I love music. It was my chosen field of study in college and led me into a career as a church organist. Music, especially traditional hymns and contemporary praise songs, comforts me and lifts my spirit more than I can express. I find comfort in the hymns because of their richness and depth. They are poetic words, based on scripture, that reflect some of my own spiritual experiences. Praise songs, by comparison, are shorter and more repetitive; they are special to me because they make God's Word come alive in a different way. Both hymns and praise songs bring me right into His presence. Either type of music reminds me to focus on the truth of the Bible rather than how I feel emotionally.

Knowing this, it seems strange when I feel depressed, that listening to music seems to be the last thing I want to do. One of the symptoms of depression is negative thinking. I hear thoughts that say nothing will help me to feel better, not even music. My friends encourage me to play a favorite recording or turn on a Christian radio station, but I can't seem to make the effort and I think of all kinds of reasons why it won't help. The truth is, the times I feel this way are the times I most need to hear the hymns and praise songs. Music is "good medicine" for my soul.

Sometimes I find it very soothing to listen to instrumental music. It seems to go beyond words to express the very groaning of my spirit. There is a local Christian radio station that broadcasts two hours of uninterrupted instrumental praise and worship music every evening. As I listen to the radio, the negative thoughts seem to fade.

When I have little motivation to read my Bible or even pray, the small effort of turning on the stereo to listen to Christian hymns and praise songs has a miraculous effect. Words of scripture sound different when they are sung rather than read. The music itself brings me right into the presence of Jesus where I feel encouraged, uplifted and re-motivated to combat the negative thoughts.

Music reminds me I am a child of God and I am loved! Although the feelings of depression may linger, I realize yet again that God's truth and His promises are more important. God has sworn to always love me, no matter how I feel, or even if I am unable to feel His love.

Here's an example of one of my favorite praise songs:

Rock of My Salvation
(Based on Isaiah 51:1.)
Words and music by Teresa Muller.
© 1982 Maranatha! Music.

You are the Rock of my salvation,
You are the strength of my life.
You are my hope and inspiration,
Lord, unto You will I cry.

I believe in You, believe in You,
For Your faithful love to me.
You have been my help in time of need;
Lord, unto You will I cleave.

~ Prayer ~
Dear Jesus, Thank You for the gift of music. Thank You for how it lifts up my down-trodden soul. Remind me to put music into my life when I'm in the dark and lonely places, so that I may be lifted up once again.

I will praise you, O LORD, with all my heart;
I will tell of all your wonders.
Psalm 9:1

I will praise the LORD as long as I live;
I will sing praises to my God
all my life long.
Psalm 146:2

Let everything that has breath
praise the LORD.
Praise the LORD.
Psalm 150:6

Comfort

14

*In Family
and Friends*

When my husband, Mel, says he is going out of town on a ministry event for the weekend, one of my first thoughts is "But, what about me? Who will take care of me?" It's a purely selfish thought and unfounded, too. Every evening and on the weekends, I depend on Mel to undress me, put me in bed, and, in the middle of the night to change my position in bed. He has never left town or even gone away for the evening without making arrangements for someone to stay with me. He has been very faithful in providing for my care. Mel has been, and will always be, my primary support person.

My family members also provide comfort and support. My dad, who is now deceased, used to keep up on the latest news about MS. He was heartbroken to see my health fail. My mother, who is in her 80's, still comes from five hundred miles away about seven times a year to visit me and my two siblings who live in a nearby city. When she stays with me, she expends an amazing amount of energy completing projects for me. It seems ironic that she should be helping her fifty-some year old daughter at a time in her life when she might rightfully expect me to care for her.

My sister and brother-in-law, both working in the medical field, are there at my call to provide counsel concerning various medical decisions I must make. My brother, who is a pastor, is a great encourager. He provides me with much appreciated support. Mel's family also supports me with their prayers. Even more important, they have been there for Mel when he has needed encouragement. Maintaining friendships is not easy as MS progresses. Dates with girlfriends or couples have been hindered by my being in a wheelchair and unable to feed myself. I wonder if it is uncomfortable for them to see me now compared to how I used to be. Meals together have often been an important part of socializing, but knowing I'm unable to feed myself may cause some to hesitate in getting together. My friends may wonder how to interact with me now. Since my activities have been severely limited, we have less in common to share. Despite these hurdles, I know that I still need companionship. I am so thankful that I belong to a church family. God knows the temptation for me to feel lonely. He always seems to find a way to bring someone to see me at just the right time.

A special friend has been coming to visit every week or so to pray with and encourage me for several years now. In the beginning it was more one-sided, but over time we have shared mutually our joys and concerns. I'll never know how a couple from church found out that I love salmon. They started coming on Saturday evenings whenever Mel was away to prepare a scrumptious meal and share it with me. We found we had some common interests, particularly in studying and playing the organ and piano. I loved to listen to her play my otherwise silent piano. They seemed to go out of their way to find special opportunities to connect with me.

One Friday evening when Mel was traveling, two teenage boys and their dad came to spend the evening with me. They made me a spaghetti supper, ate with me, and entertained me through the evening with piano playing, funny stories and laughter. A very active woman from church, who had a recurrence of cancer and had been transferred to a hospice center, called me one day to see if I would be interested in getting together with her and two other women with MS and cancer. After an initial meeting all together, she and I decided to continue to meet weekly for prayer. As her cancer progressed, we had to exchange face-to-face contact for telephone conversations. It was a blessing for me to count her as my friend, as well as to be able to pray for her, giving me a sense of purpose, an outlet to minister to someone else rather than always being the one receiving ministry.

My husband noticed it was becoming increasingly difficult for me to manage our household bookkeeping. He asked a woman who worked for him at his office if she would be willing to help me. She has been invaluable to me ever since she took over my responsibility on a weekly basis. You may not have family near enough and willing to spend time with you. Perhaps you have also experienced the loss of friendships. If you have no other group affiliations, you may find a wonderful world of support in attending a support group. Some support groups are designed for a specific condition or disability – like MS, in my case. Other support groups are less specific. They all provide an opportunity to come together with others living with a common challenge or need to share and compare experiences. Sometimes, group members are able to understand each other far better than an outsider might, having been there themselves. Whether your support system is formal or informal, friends, family members, or other patients, I have found that we really do need people in our lives who are willing to share themselves with us and to allow us to minister in some way to them.

"God never meant for us to face the tough times alone; that's why He gave us each other."   (Taken from a greeting card I received from a friend.)

When I am in need of refreshment, it isn't easy to think of the needs of others. But I have found that if, instead of praying for my own comfort and satisfaction, I ask the Lord to enable me to give to others, an amazing thing often happens –I find my own needs wonderfully met.   Elisabeth Elliot

~ Prayer ~
Gracious Father, thank You for the gift of family and friends. You created us as relational beings; we really do need each other.

He who refreshes others will himself be refreshed.
Proverbs 11:25

A friend loves at all times, and a brother is
born for adversity.
Proverbs 17:17

Though one may be overpowered, two can defend
themselves. A cord of three strands is not quickly broken.
Ecclesiastes 4:12

Comfort

15

In Seeing
The Unseen

"Life is a journey that's homeward bound," reads a plaque on my dressing room wall. It was a gift I gave to my grandmother late in her life, to remind her of the eternal home prepared for her. After her death, the plaque I had given her was returned to me, a reminder to me of the home where I am headed when I leave this world. I see it every day and it never fails to encourage me.

The continual set backs of MS are discouraging. Each day of the future can seem more hopeless than the last. When I start to wonder how much more of this I can take, I turn to Paul's letter to the Corinthians where he says:

"Therefore we do not lose heart. Though outwardly we are wasting away, yet inwardly we are being renewed day by day. For our light and momentary troubles are achieving for us an eternal glory that far outweighs them all. So we fix our eyes not on what is seen, but on what is unseen. For what is seen is temporary, but what is unseen is eternal." (2 Corinthians 4:16-18) This is one of my favorite passages in the Bible. Paul reminds me not to give in to feeling discouraged or hopeless. When those feelings come up, he suggests that I "fix my eyes on what is unseen."   It's not hard for me to come up with a list of what I see, but to find what is unseen, I look to the Bible.

What Is Seen: What Is Unseen:
My sick useless body   A new body made by God!

How Do I Know?   *Now we know that if the earthly tent we live in is destroyed, we have a building from God,*

an eternal house in heaven, not built by human hands.
2 Corinthians 5:1

What Is Seen: What Is Unseen:
Suffering   Relief From Suffering!

How Do I Know?   *…Give relief to you who are troubled,*
and to us as well. This will happen when the Lord Jesus
is revealed from heaven in blazing fire with his powerful angels.
2 Thessalonians 1:7

What Is Seen: What Is Unseen:
Tears, Pain and Grief   No More!

How Do I Know?   *He will wipe every tear from their eyes.*
There will be no more death or mourning or crying or pain,
for the old order of things has passed away.
Revelation 21:4

What Is Seen: What Is Unseen:
Sorrow and Sadness   No More Feeling Sad!

How Do I Know?   *Gladness and joy will overtake them,*
and sorrow and sighing will flee away.
Isaiah 35:10

What Is Seen: What Is Unseen:
Eventual Death   Death Will Be Destroyed and
God will give us eternal life!

How Do I Know? *For my Father's will is that*
everyone who looks to the Son and believes in him
shall have eternal life and I will raise him up the last day.
John 6:40

As a believer in Jesus Christ, I have no reason to fear death. Each physical loss is a reminder that my life here is temporary. I am "homeward bound" and home, for me, is to be with God in eternity. This suffering will pass and be completely forgotten in the joyous reunion that is to come. As for now, I wait. I fix my eyes on things unseen, on the life to come. I remember God's promises for my future.

God wants to transform every form of human suffering into something glorious. He can bring life out of death.   Elisabeth Elliot

~ Prayer ~
Eternal Father, thank You for the reassurance that You have given me that my life
now is just a journey to my eternal home with You. Thank you that there will be no
more suffering, sorrow or pain. Come, LORD Jesus!

For I know the plans I have for you, declares
the LORD, "plans to prosper you and not to harm you,
plans to give you hope and a future.
Jeremiah 29:11

*"Do not let your hearts be troubled. Trust in
God, trust also in me. In my Father's house are many
rooms ...I am going there to prepare a place for you...
I will come back and will take you to be with me
that you also may be where I am."*
John 14:1-3

*Christ Jesus who died – more than that, who
was raised to life – is at the right hand of God and
is interceding for us.*
Romans 8:34

Comfort **16**

In The Truth

For those of us who have multiple sclerosis, and others who have experienced life-threatening illnesses, we often wrestle with the physical changes that cause us to question our purpose for living. For me, God's truth brings comfort to my life daily as I face physical and emotional challenges.

No matter what I face, I know that God loves me. My faith has sustained me over the years. I was raised by godly parents who loved me and taught me to trust the truth in God's holy word. When my faith is tried or I begin to question my circumstances, I find comfort in God's word.

When I wonder, "Who am I?" God's truth says, "How great is the love the Father has lavished on us, that we should be called children of God! And that is what we are!" (1 John 3:1)

When I wonder about my purpose, the Bible tells me, "For we are God's workmanship, created in Christ Jesus to do good works, which God prepared in advance for us to do. (Eph. 2:10)

These truths applied to my life when I was a child. They applied to me before I was diagnosed with MS. They still apply to my life now though I have been rendered completely helpless and physically incapacitated. Comfort for me is knowing that God's truth revealed through the holy scriptures will never fail me.

~ Prayer ~
Dear Heavenly Father, thank You that You are the Absolute Truth for me to cling to. Help me to measure every circumstance that touches my life against the absolute that You are the truth.

Show me your ways, O Lord, teach me your
paths; guide me in your truth and teach me, for you
are God my Savior.
Psalm 24:4

"Then you will experience for yourselves the
truth, and the truth will free you."
John 8:32

And now you also have heard the truth, the
Good News that God saves you. And when you believed
in Christ, He identified you as His own...
Ephesians 1:13

Comfort 17

In Finding The Blessing

Do you wonder how there could ever be a blessing that comes from having a debilitating illness like multiple sclerosis? Finding out that you have a life-threatening illness, experiencing changes and losses one after another, year after year, you may wonder why this happened to you. It may seem impossible to consider that good could come from your suffering. Yet, God is able and willing to do exactly that. I know, because He is creating good from my brokenness and blessing through my illness. In the past I was a very orderly, organized person. I've always enjoyed keeping my surroundings neat and clean with a place to store each item and an efficient method for completing each task. Unfortunately, over time I let this part of my life take precedence over other aspects of who I am. A great deal of my energy and thinking was consumed by it. I was so caught up in the tasks that I found it difficult to relax. I didn't allow myself to "have fun." Worse, when we invited people to our home I couldn't let myself enjoy their company. I was too preoccupied with anything I might have left undone. My husband would remind me, "Jane, people are more important than things," and I would agree with him. But I wouldn't change, because in my heart I didn't want to let go.

As the symptoms of MS depleted my energy and limited my mobility, in frustration I thought, "I can't give my ways up; that's not me. This is the way I am; I can't change the way I am." One day my husband confronted me saying, "Jane, you're as bad as the drunk in the gutter who says, 'I can't change!' He thinks he will always be an alcoholic. You're saying God can't change the way you are. This is the way you will always be." I knew what he said was true. It was MS that forced me to begin to change. I was losing control over my movements, so that it was becoming impossible for me to continue my old, obsessive behaviors. God used my illness to begin transforming my beliefs. He showed me how He would have things be if He could have His way in my life. He began to pry away my efforts to control my world so that He could reveal to me the greater blessings He had in store for me.

Maybe you, like I, have heard the following words before, "And we know that in all things God works for good for those who love Him, who have been called according to His purpose" (Romans 8:28). It's not that God causes bad things to happen, or that He allows them to happen without caring about us. And it's not that God is not powerful enough to stop bad things from happening. I believe that God's love for us is so much bigger than anything we are able to understand, that sometimes His plan for blessing can only come from the experience of suffering. Who will receive the benefit from God's work? The verse says "those who love God ... who are called according to His purpose." Who are the ones called according to His purpose? We are! You are and I am. God chose ALL people to be His. Who are the ones who love Him? I can't answer that for you, but I know that I love Him with all my heart. I believe that He loves you and He is working out a blessing for you just as He is, and has, for me. Trust Him. When we look with eyes of faith, we will see all the blessings He is longing to give us.

Repeatedly throughout our lives we encounter the roadblock of suffering.
What do we do with it? Our answer will determine what we can say to another
who needs comfort.

Elisabeth Elliot

~ Prayer ~
Dear Jesus, thank you that all things are possible with You. It is your strength
that gives me the power to change so that I will experience Your blessings.
In Jesus' name.

So do not fear, for I am with you; do not be dismayed,
for I am your God. I will strengthen you and
help you; I will uphold you with my righteous right hand.
Isaiah 41:10

Praise be to the God and Father of our LORD
Jesus Christ, who has blessed us in the heavenly
realms with every spiritual blessing in Christ.
For he chose us in him before the creation of the world
to be holy and blameless in his sight.
Ephesians 1:3-4

…For it is God who works in you to will and
to act according to his good purpose.
Philippians 2:13

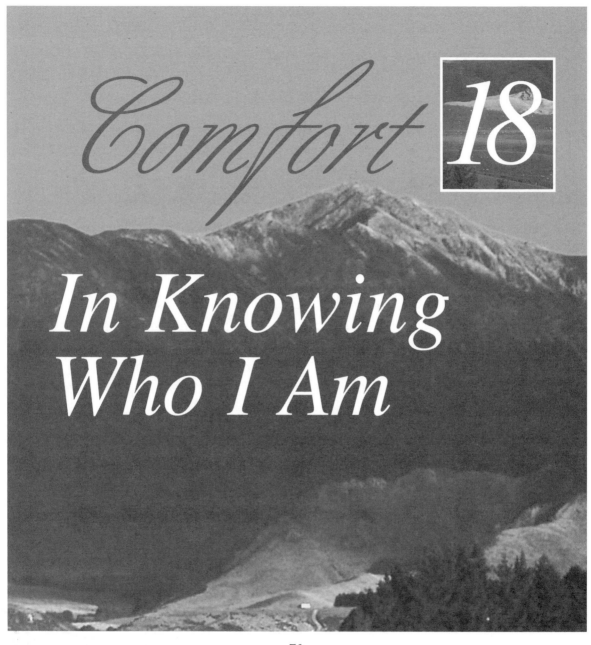

Comfort 18

In Knowing Who I Am

Looking back on my life, I don't think I realized how much I had come to depend on my ability to "do" things to strengthen my sense of value and worth. It's a fairly common belief among people of varying generations and nationalities. What we "do" in life becomes our definition of who we are. He is a fisherman. She is an engineer. He is a football player. She is a seamstress. He is a Boy Scout leader. She is a pilot. I could be defined by my roles as homemaker, church organist, business manager, and so on. In other words, the "who I am" (a state of being) was defined by "what I do" (an act of doing.)

What happens for people like you and me when our bodies and minds deteriorate, and we are no longer able to "do," all the things we used to do? Gradually becoming less able to "do" I found myself wandering down a doom-filled path of frustration, resentment and depression.

Thankfully, God reminded me of a truth I have always known, a more constant and stable truth. Knowing "who I am" is my source and foundation for defining my value and worth. What I "do" is merely a result of who I am. So, how do we come to know who we are? The Bible tells us that God chose us to be His, even before He created the world! (Ephesians 1:4) It says from the very beginning He planned to adopt us and make us members of His family, inheritors of all that is His! (Ephesians 1:5). According to these verses, the question is not "who we are" but "whose we are."

We are God's precious children, not because of anything we have done, but simply because He created us for His good pleasure. He made us His own, precisely because of His everlasting love. What that means for you and me is that we may be assured of our value and worth despite the fact that we are having to give up the activities we used to do. As my body succumbs to MS, I find great comfort in knowing whose I am. This same comfort is offered to you, as well.

Be persuaded timid soul, that He has loved you too much to cease loving you.

Archbishop Fenelon (as quoted by Elisabeth Eliot)

~ Prayer ~
Dear God, thank You that I am deeply loved by You for who I am and not what I do.
Help me keep my eyes fixed on You.

Know that the LORD is God. It is He that made us,
and we are His; we are His people and the sheep of his pastures.
Psalm 100:3

How great is the love the Father has lavished on us,
that we should be called children of God! And that is what we are!
I John 3:1

We know that we live in him and he in us,
because he has given us of his Spirit.
I John 4:13

GOD desires to give you Comfort in the Journey

My dear friend, what about you? Have you been able to find comfort in your journey? I know it is hard when you struggle physically and emotionally. Maybe you just received news of your illness. No matter what your condition is right now or what you are facing in the future, God desires to take your hand and be there in the midst of your feelings of despair and hopelessness.

I want so much for you to know Jesus who will never leave or forsake you. He promises you a new body and the opportunity to live with Him forever in heaven.

We all must come to Him by faith. We must believe that he is the God who created the universe. The Bible is true and reveals the true source of our encouragement and hope.

Will you come by faith and pray this simple prayer? "Lord Jesus, I repent of my sins and rebellion against Your will. I ask You to forgive me. I ask You to come into my heart and make Your residence there. I want to know Your comfort in my journey. Fill me Lord with Your Holy Spirit that I might understand Your holy word. Thank You for dying for my sins. I love You Lord Jesus, Amen."

If you prayed that prayer please write me and seek out someone you know who loves the Lord! Tell them that you surrendered your heart to the Lord Jesus. Then seek out a Bible-believing church and begin to attend worship services and Bible study. This will help you grow in your faith.

God loves you and will always be there with you even when you do not sense Him in the journey.

"Never will I leave you; never will I forsake you."   Hebrews 13:5

You may contact Jane Goebel at:
    www.comfortforthejourney.org or www.impactlife.org

Impact for Life Ministries
1107 Garden of Gods Road
Colorado Springs, CO 80907

Jane's Song

I look forward to a future day
When Jane will be in God's presence;
And before all the hosts of His heavenly realm,
To her, He will extend His hand.
He will raise her up,
On her feet she'll stand firm;
One step, then two she'll be dancing.
He will lead her with sweeps,
And swirls and leaps. He will lift her and call out
her name –

"My most beautiful bride
Welcome home, welcome home.
Time has come for feasting and laughter.
Let us sing with joy, for you are now whole.
I have saved you from death, precious Jane,
To be mine forever."

And her face will light up,
How her eyes will sparkle
How agile her body will be!
No more tears, no more sighs,
With strong voice she will sing,

Like the angels her praises will ring.
One step, then two, she'll be dancing with God.
All will join in rejoicing.
The trumpets will sound
And praises resound
In honor of the King
And the glory of His bride;
She's the apple of His eye.

We wait patiently for that future day
Making most of the time He has given
Knowing He has a purpose for biding His time
Trusting His love for Jane
Is greater than mine
Thanking You Lord for every breath that she takes
As she prepares for that Glorious future day!

Written for Jane by Kari Dahlin, 2005:

Jane's Favorite Psalm

O LORD, you have searched me and you know me. You know when I sit and when I rise; you perceive my thoughts from afar. You discern my going out and my lying down; you are familiar with all my ways.

Before a word is on my tongue you know it completely, O LORD.

You hem me in - behind and before; you have laid your hand upon me. Such knowledge is too wonderful for me, too lofty for me to attain.

Where can I go from your Spirit? Where can I flee from your presence? If I go up to the heavens, you are there; if I make my bed in the depths, you are there. If I rise on the wings of the dawn, if I settle on the far side of the sea, even there your hand will guide me, your right hand will hold me fast.

If I say, "Surely the darkness will hide me and the light become night around me," even the darkness will not be dark to you; the night will shine like the day, for darkness is as light to you.

For you created my inmost being; you knit me together in my mother's womb. I praise you because I am fearfully and wonderfully made; your works are wonderful, I know that full well. My frame was not hidden from you when I was made in the secret place. When I was woven together in the depths of the earth, your eyes saw my unformed body.

All the days ordained for me were written in your book before one of them came to be.

How precious to me are your thoughts, O God! How vast is the sum of them! Were I to count them, they would outnumber the grains of sand. When I awake, I am still with you.

If only you would slay the wicked, O God! Away from me, you bloodthirsty men! They speak of you with evil intent; your adversaries misuse your name. Do I not hate those who hate you, O LORD, and abhor those who rise up against you? I have nothing but hatred for them; I count them my enemies.

Search me, O God, and know my heart; test me and know my anxious thoughts. See if there is any offensive way in me, and lead me in the way everlasting.
Psalm 139

Comforting Scriptures For the Journey

ADVERSITY

The LORD is good, a refuge in times of trouble. He cares for those who trust in him.
Nahum 1:7

The LORD is a refuge for the oppressed, a stronghold in times of trouble.
Psalm 9:9

The LORD is my rock, my fortress and my deliverer; my God is my rock, in whom I take refuge. He is my shield and the horn of my salvation, my stronghold.
Psalm 18:2

You, O LORD, keep my lamp burning; my God turns my darkness into light.
Psalm 18:28

For he has not despised or disdained the suffering of the afflicted one; he has not hidden his face from him but has listened to his cry for help. Psalm 22:24

Love the LORD, all his saints! The LORD preserves the faithful, but the proud he pays back in full.
Psalm 31:23

You are my hiding place; you will protect me from trouble and surround me with songs of deliverance.
Psalm 32:7

A righteous man may have many troubles, but the LORD delivers him from them all.
Psalm 34:19

If the LORD delights in a man's way, he makes his steps firm; though he stumble, he will not fall, for the LORD upholds him with his hand. Psalm 37:23-24

The salvation of the righteous comes from the LORD; he is their stronghold in time of trouble.   Psalm 37:39

Why are you downcast, my soul? Why so disturbed within me? Put your hope in God, for I will yet praise him, my Savior and my God. Psalm 42:11

My flesh and my heart may fail, but God is the strength of my heart and my portion forever.   Psalm 73:26

If you make the Most High your dwelling-even the LORD, who is my refuge-then no harm will befall you, no disaster will come near your tent.   For he will command his angels concerning you to guard you in all your ways; they will lift you up in their hands, so that you will not strike your foot against a stone. Psalm 91:9-12

Those who sow in tears will reap with songs of joy. He who goes out weeping, carrying seed to sow, will return with songs of joy, carrying sheaves with him.
                                    Psalm 126:5-6

Though I walk in the midst of trouble, you preserve my life; you stretch out your hand against the anger of my foes, with your right hand you save me.
                                    Psalm 138:7

I have told you these things, so that in me you may have peace. In this world you will have trouble. But take heart! I have overcome the world.
                                    John 16:33

ASSURANCE

Know that the LORD has set apart the godly for himself; the LORD will hear when I call to him.   Psalm 4:3

The Spirit himself testifies with our spirit that we are God's children.
                                                                Romans 8:16

For I am convinced that neither death nor life, neither angels nor demons, neither the present nor the future, nor any powers, neither height nor depth, nor anything else in all creation, will be able to separate us from the love of God that is in Christ Jesus our LORD.   Romans 8:38-39

In him and through faith in him we may approach God with freedom and confidence.
                                                                Ephesians 3:12

That is why I am suffering as I am. Yet I am not ashamed, because I know whom I have believed, and am convinced that he is able to guard what I have entrusted to him for that day.   2 Timothy 1:12

We have come to share in Christ if we hold firmly till the end the confidence we had at first.   Hebrews 3:14

Let us draw near to God with a sincere heart in full assurance of faith, having our hearts sprinkled to cleanse us from a guilty conscience and having our bodies washed with pure water.   Hebrews 10:22

Now faith is being sure of what we hope for and certain of what we do not see.
                                                                Hebrews 11:1

DEPRESSION

How long, O LORD? Will you forget me forever? How long will you hide your face from me? How long must I wrestle with my thoughts and every day have sorrow in my heart?   Psalm 13:1-2

But I trust in your unfailing love; my heart rejoices in your salvation. I will sing to the LORD, for he has been good to me.   Psalm 13:5-6

In my distress I called to the LORD; I cried to my God for help.   Psalm 18:6

You, O LORD, keep my lamp burning; my God turns my darkness into light.   Psalm 18:28

I will be glad and rejoice in your love, for you saw my affliction and knew the anguish of my soul.   Psalm 31:7

The righteous cry out and the LORD hears them; he delivers them from all their troubles. The LORD is close to the brokenhearted and saves those who are crushed in spirit. A righteous man may have many troubles, but the LORD delivers him from them all.   Psalm 34:17-19

Why are you downcast, O my soul? Why so disturbed within me? Put your hope in God, for I will yet praise him, my Savior and my God.   Psalm 42:5-6

Trouble and distress have come upon me, but your commands are my delight.   Psalm 119:143

Then you will call, and the LORD will answer: "Here am I."   Isaiah 58:9

DISCOURAGEMENT

The LORD is my light and my salvation-whom shall I fear? The LORD is the stronghold of my life-of whom shall I be afraid? When evil men advance against me to devour my flesh, when my enemies and my foes attack me, they will stumble and fall.   Psalm 27:1-2

Be strong and take heart, all you who hope in the LORD.
                                                                     Psalm 31:24

Though I walk in the midst of trouble, you preserve my life; you stretch out your hand against the anger of my foes, with your right hand you save me.
                                                                     Psalm 138:7

For I am the LORD, Your God, who takes hold of your hand and says to you, do not fear; I will help you.   Isaiah 41:13

The ransomed of the LORD will return. They will enter Zion with singing; everlasting joy will crown their heads. Gladness and joy will overtake them, and sorrow and sighing will flee away.   Isaiah 51:11

Do not let your hearts be troubled. Trust in God; trust also in me.
                                                                     John 14:1

Peace I leave with you; my peace I give you. I do not give to you as the world gives. Do not let your hearts be troubled and do not be afraid.
                                                                     John 14:27

We are hard pressed on every side, but not crushed; perplexed, but not in despair;

persecuted, but not abandoned; struck down, but not destroyed.

2 Corinthians 4:8-9

Let us not become weary in doing good, for at the proper time we will reap a harvest if we do not give up.

Galatians 6:9

Being confident of this, that he who began a good work in you will carry it on to completion until the day of Christ Jesus.

Philippians 1:6

Do not be anxious about anything, but in everything, by prayer and petition, with thanksgiving, present your requests to God. And the peace of God, which transcends all understanding, will guard your hearts and your minds in Christ Jesus. Finally, brothers, whatever is true, whatever is noble, whatever is right, whatever is pure, whatever is lovely, whatever is admirable-if anything is excellent or praiseworthy-think about such things.

Philippians 4:6-8

So do not throw away your confidence; it will be richly rewarded. You need to persevere so that when you have done the will of God, you will receive what he has promised.

Hebrews 10:35-36

In this you greatly rejoice, though now for a little while you may have had to suffer grief in all kinds of trials. These have come so that your faith-of greater worth than gold, which perishes even though refined by fire-may be proved genuine and may result in praise, glory and honor when Jesus Christ is revealed.

1 Peter 1:6-7

FAITH

"If you can?" said Jesus. "Everything is possible for him who believes."

Mark 9:23

The apostles said to the LORD, "Increase our faith!" He replied,"If you have faith as small as a mustard seed, you can say to this mulberry tree, 'Be uprooted and planted in the sea,' and it will obey you."   Luke 17:5-6

For in the gospel a righteousness from God is revealed, a righteousness that is by faith from first to last, just as it is written: "The righteous will live by faith."

Romans 1:17

This righteousness from God comes through faith in Jesus Christ to all who believe.

Romans 3:22

Therefore, since we have been justified through faith, we have peace with God through our LORD Jesus Christ, through whom we have gained access by faith into this grace in which we now stand. And we rejoice in the hope of the glory of God.

Romans 5:1-2

Consequently, faith comes from hearing the message, and the message is heard through the word of Christ.   Romans 10:17

For by the grace given me I say to every one of you: "Do not think of yourself more highly than you ought, but rather think of yourself with sober judgment, in accordance with the measure of faith God has given you.   Romans 12:3

We live by faith, not by sight.   2 Corinthians 5:7

Now faith is being sure of what we hope for and certain of what we do not see.
Hebrews 11:1

And without faith it is impossible to please God, because anyone who comes to him must believe that he exists and that he rewards those who earnestly seek him.
Hebrews 11:6

Let us fix our eyes on Jesus, the author and perfecter of our faith, who for the joy set before him endured the cross, scorning its shame, and sat down at the right hand of the throne of God.
Hebrews 12:2

What good is it, my brothers, if a man claims to have faith but has no deeds? Can such faith save him? Suppose a brother or sister is without clothes and daily food. If one of you says to him, "Go, I wish you well; keep warm and well fed," but does nothing about his physical needs, what good is it? In the same way, faith by itself, if it is not accompanied by action, is dead.
James 2:14-17

These have come so that your faith-of greater worth than gold, which perishes even though refined by fire-may be proved genuine and may result in praise, glory and honor when Jesus Christ is revealed. Though you have not seen him, you love him; and even though you do not see him now, you believe in him and are filled with an inexpressible and glorious joy, for you are receiving the goal of your faith, the salvation of your souls.
1 Peter 1:7-9

For everyone born of God overcomes the world. This is the victory that has overcome the world, even our faith.
1 John 5:4

FEAR

Even though I walk through the valley of the shadow of death, I will fear no evil, for you are with me; your rod and your staff, they comfort me. You prepare a table before me in the presence of my enemies. You anoint my head with oil; my cup overflows.
                                                                    Psalm 23:4-5

The LORD is my light and my salvation-whom shall I fear? The LORD is the stronghold of my life-of whom shall I be afraid? Though an army besiege me, my heart will not fear; though war break out against me, even then will I be confident.
                                                                    Psalm 27:1, 3

Be strong and take heart, all you who hope in the LORD.
                                                                    Psalm 31:24

In God I trust; I will not be afraid. What can man do to me?
                                                                    Psalm 56:11

He who dwells in the shelter of the Most High will rest in the shadow of the Almighty.
                                                                    Psalm 91:1

He will cover you with his feathers, and under his wings you will find refuge; his faithfulness will be your shield and rampart. You will not fear the terror of night, nor the arrow that flies by day, nor the pestilence that stalks in the darkness, nor the plague that destroys at midday. A thousand may fall at your side, ten thousand at your right hand, but it will not come near you.   Psalm 91:4-7

Then no harm will befall you, no disaster will come near your tent. For he will command his angels concerning you to guard you in all your ways.
                                                                    Psalm 91:10-11

Have no fear of sudden disaster or of the ruin that overtakes the wicked, for the LORD will be your confidence and will keep your foot from being snared.

Proverbs 3:25-26

In righteousness you will be established: Tyranny will be far from you; you will have nothing to fear. Terror will be far removed; it will not come near you.

Isaiah 54:14

Peace I leave with you; my peace I give you. I do not give to you as the world gives. Do not let your hearts be troubled and do not be afraid.

John 14:27

For you did not receive a spirit that makes you a slave again to fear, but you received the Spirit of sonship. And by him we cry, "Abba, Father."

Romans 8:15

For God did not give us a spirit of timidity, but a spirit of power, of love and of self-discipline.   2 Timothy 1:7

There is no fear in love. But perfect love drives out fear, because fear has to do with punishment. The one who fears is not made perfect in love.

1 John 4:18

GUIDANCE

He restores my soul. He guides me in paths of righteousness for his name's sake.
Psalm 23:3

I will instruct you and teach you in the way you should go; I will counsel you and watch over you. Psalm 32:8

If the LORD delights in a man's way, he makes his steps firm; though he stumble, he will not fall, for the LORD upholds him with his hand. Psalm 37:23-24

How can a young man keep his way pure? By living according to your word.
Psalm 119:9

I have hidden your word in my heart that I might not sin against you.
Psalm 119:11

Your statutes are my delight; they are my counselors.
Psalm 119:24

Your word is a lamp to my feet and a light for my path.
Psalm 119:105

When you walk, they will guide you; when you sleep, they will watch over you; when you awake, they will speak to you. For these commands are a lamp, this teaching is a light, and the corrections of discipline are the way to life.
Proverbs 6:22-23

Do not let this book of the law depart from your mouth; meditate on it day and night, so that you may be careful to do everything written in it. Then you will be prosperous and successful. Joshua 1:8

Whether you turn to the right or to the left, your ears will hear a voice behind you, saying, "this is the way; walk in it." Isaiah 30:21

To the Jews who had believed him, Jesus said, "If you hold to my teaching, you are really my disciples. Then you will know the truth, and the truth will set you free." John 8:31-32

All scripture is God-breathed and is useful for teaching, rebuking, correcting and training in righteousness, so that the man of God may be thoroughly equipped for every good work. 2 Timothy 3:16-17

PATIENCE

Wait for the LORD; be strong and take heart and wait for the LORD. Psalm 27:14

Be still before the LORD and wait patiently for him; do not fret when men succeed in their ways, when they carry out their wicked schemes. Refrain from anger and turn from wrath; do not fret-it leads only to evil. For evil men will be cut off, but those who hope in the LORD will inherit the land. Psalm 37:7-9

I waited patiently for the LORD; he turned to me and heard my cry. Psalm 40:1

The end of a matter is better than its beginning, and patience is better than pride. Do not be quickly provoked in your spirit, for anger resides in the lap of fools.

Ecclesiastes 7:8-9

...but those who hope in the LORD will renew their strength. They will soar on wings like eagles; they will run and not grow weary, they will walk and not be faint.

Isaiah 40:31

Not only so, but we also rejoice in our sufferings, because we know that suffering produces perseverance; perseverance, character; and character, hope. And hope does not disappoint us, because God has poured out his love into our hearts by the Holy Spirit, whom he has given us.

Romans 5:3-5

But if we hope for what we do not yet have, we wait for it patiently.

Romans 8:25

For everything that was written in the past was written to teach us, so that through endurance and the encouragement of the scriptures we might have hope. May the God who gives endurance and encouragement give you a spirit of unity among yourselves as you follow Christ Jesus.

Romans 15:4-5

But the fruit of the Spirit is love, joy, peace, patience, kindness, goodness, faithfulness, gentleness, and self control.

Galatians 5:22-23

We do not want you to become lazy, but to imitate those who through faith and patience inherit what has been promised.

Hebrews 6:12

So do not throw away your confidence; it will be richly rewarded. You need to persevere so that when you have done the will of God, you will receive what he has promised. For in just a very little while, "He who is coming will come and will not delay."

Hebrews 10:35-37

Therefore, since we are surrounded by such a great cloud of witnesses, let us throw off everything that hinders and the sin that so easily entangles, and let us run with perseverance the race marked out for us.   Hebrews 12:1

Consider it pure joy, my brothers, whenever you face trials of many kinds, because you know that the testing of your faith develops perserverence. Perseverance must finish its work so that you may be mature and complete, not lacking anything.
                                                                        James 1:3-4

Be patient, then, brothers, until the LORD'S coming. See how the farmer waits for the land to yield its valuable crop and how patient he is for the autumn and spring rains. You too, be patient and stand firm, because the LORD'S coming is near.
                                                                        James 5:7-8

PRAYER

"You will pray to him, and he will hear you, and you will fulfill your vows.
                                                                        Job 22:27

I will extol the LORD at all times; his praise will always be on my lips. My soul will boast in the LORD; let the afflicted hear and rejoice. Glorify the LORD with me; let us exalt his name together. I sought the LORD, and he answered me; he delivered me from all my fears.   Psalm 34; 1-4

Evening, morning and noon I cry out in distress, and he hears my voice.
                                                                        Psalm 55:17

He will call upon me, and I will answer him; I will be with him in trouble, I will deliver him and honor him.
                                          Psalm 91:15

The LORD is near to all who call on him, to all who call on him in truth. He fulfills the desires of those who fear him; he hears their cry and saves them.
                                          Psalm 145:18-19

The LORD is far from the wicked but he hears the prayer of the righteous.
                                          Proverbs 15:29

Then you will call, and the LORD will answer; you will cry for help, and he will say: "Here am I."
                                          Isaiah 58:9

Before they call I will answer; while they are still speaking I will hear.
                                          Isaiah 65:24

Then you will call upon me and come and pray to me, and I will listen to you.
                                          Jeremiah 29:12

Call to me and I will answer you and tell you great and unsearchable things you do not know.
                                          Jeremiah 33:3

But when you pray, go into your room, close the door and pray to your Father, who is unseen. Then your Father, who sees what is done in secret, will reward you.
                                          Matthew 6:6

Do not be like them, for your Father knows what you need before you ask him.
                                          Matthew 6:8

Ask and it will be given to you; seek and you will find; knock and the door will be opened to you. For everyone who asks receives; he who seeks finds; and to him who knocks, the door will be opened.   Matthew 7:7-8

If you, then, though you are evil, know how to give good gifts to your children, how much more will your Father in heaven give good gifts to those who ask him!   Matthew 7:11

Therefore confess your sins to each other and pray for each other so that you may be healed. The prayer of a righteous man is powerful and effective.   James 5:16

Dear friends, if our hearts do not condemn us, we have confidence before God and receive from him anything we ask, because we obey his commands and do what pleases him.   1 John 3:21-22

This is the confidence we have in approaching God: that if we ask anything according to his will, he hears us. And if we know that he hears us-whatever we ask-we know that we have what we asked of him.   1 John 5:14-15

STABILITY

Praise be to the LORD, who has given rest to his people Israel just as he promised. Not one word has failed of all the good promises he gave through his servant Moses.   1 Kings 8:56

He lifted me out of the slimy pit, out of the mud and mire; he set my feet on a rock and gave me a firm place to stand.   Psalm 40:2

God is our refuge and strength, an ever-present help in trouble.

Psalm 46:1

Your word, O LORD, is eternal; it stands firm in the heavens.

Psalm 119:80

My son, pay attention to what I say; listen closely to my words. Do not let them out of your sight, keep them within your heart; for they are life to those who find them and health to a man's whole body.　　　Proverbs 4:20-22

The name of the LORD is a strong tower; the righteous run to it and are safe.

Proverbs 18:10

The grass withers and the flowers fall, but the word of our God stands forever.

Isaiah 40:8

I tell you the truth, until heaven and earth disappear, not the smallest letter, not the least stroke of a pen, will by any means disappear from the Law until everything is accomplished.　　　Matthew 5:18

Heaven and earth will pass away, but my words will never pass away.

Matthew 24:35

What, then, shall we say in response to this? If God is for us, who can be against us?　　　Romans 8:31

But the LORD is faithful, and he will strengthen and protect you from the evil one.

2 Thessalonians 3:3

For you have been born again, not of perishable seed, but of imperishable, through the living and enduring word of God. For, "All men are like grass, and all their glory is like the flowers of the field; the grass withers and the flowers fall, but the word of the LORD stands forever." And this is the word that was preached to you.

1 Peter 1:23-25

To him who is able to keep you from falling and to present you before his glorious presence without fault and with great joy- to the only God our Savior be glory, majesty, power and authority, through Jesus Christ our LORD, before all ages, now and forevermore! Amen.

Jude 24-25

STRENGTH

I love you, O LORD, my strength. The LORD is my rock and my fortress and my deliverer, my God is my rock, in whom I take refuge. He is my shield and my horn of salvation, my stronghold. I call to the LORD, who is worthy of praise, and I am saved from my enemies.

Psalm 18:1-3

My soul is weary with sorrow; be gracious to me through your law.

Psalm 119:28

So do not fear, for I am with you; do not be dismayed, for I am your God. I will strengthen you and help you; I will uphold you with my righteous right hand.

Isaiah 41:10

How can I, your servant, talk with you my LORD? My strength is gone and I can hardly breathe. " Do not be afraid, O man highly esteemed," he said. Peace! Be strong now; be strong."

Daniel 10:17, 19

I pray that out of his glorious riches he may strengthen you with power through his spirit in your inner being, so that Christ may dwell in your hearts through faith. And I pray that you, being rooted and established in love, may have power with all the saints.   Ephesians 3: 16-17

Finally, be strong in the LORD and in his mighty power.   Ephesians 6: 10

Yes, and I ask you, loyal yokefellow, help these women who have contended at my side in the cause of the gospel, along with Clement and the rest of my fellow workers, whose names are in the book of life.   Philippians 4: 13

WEAKNESS

Wait for the Lord; be strong and take heart and wait for the LORD. We wait in hope for the LORD; he is our help and our shield.
                                                        Psalm 33: 20

May the peoples praise you, O God; may all the peoples praise you.
                                                        Psalm 67:5

I wait for the LORD, my soul waits, and in his word I put my hope.
                                                        Psalm 130: 5

The LORD will fulfill his purpose for me; your love, O LORD, endures forever -- do not abandon the works of your hands.   Psalm 138: 38

For my thoughts are not your thoughts, neither are your ways my ways, declares the LORD.
                                                                                    Isaiah 55: 8

Let us consider how we may spur one another on toward love and good deeds.
                                                                                    Hebrews 10: 23

WISDOM

Look to the LORD and his strength; seek his face always.
                                                                                    1 Chronicles 16:11

Who, then, is the man that fears the LORD? He will instruct him in the way chosen for him.
                                                                                    Psalm 25:12

I will instruct you and teach you in the way you should go; I will counsel you and watch over you.
                                                                                    Psalm 32:8

Trust in the LORD with all your heart and lean not on your own understanding; in all your ways acknowledge him, and he will make your paths straight.
                                                                                    Proverbs 3:5-6

For the LORD gives wisdom, and from his mouth come knowledge and understanding. He holds victory in store for the upright, he is a shield to those whose walk is blameless, for he guards the course of the just and protects the way of his faithful ones. Then you will understand what is right and just and fair-every good path.
                                                                                    Proverbs 6-9

For lack of guidance a nation falls, but many advisers make victory sure. Plans fail for lack of counsel, but with many advisers they succeed.

Proverbs 15:22

A wise man has great power, and a man of knowledge increases strength; for waging war you need guidance, and for victory many advisers.

Proverbs 24:5-6

Call to me and I will answer you and tell you great and unsearchable things you do not know.

Jeremiah 33:3

But seek first his kingdom and his righteousness, and all these things will be given to you as well.

Matthew 6:33

For it is God who works in you to will and to act according to his good purpose.

Philippians 2:13

That is why I am suffering as I am. Yet I am not ashamed, because I know whom I have believed, and am convinced that he is able to guard what I have entrusted to him for that day.

2 Timothy 1:12

If any of you lacks wisdom, he should ask God, who gives generously to all without finding fault, and it will be given to him.

James 1:5

Acknowledgements

1. "My Hope Is Built on Nothing Less" text by Edward Mote (1787-1874) Public Domain

2. All Elisabeth Elliot quotes used by permission of author Keep A Quiet Heart © 1995 by Elisabeth Elliot, A Lamp for My Feet © 1985 by Elisabeth Elliot, Love has a Price Tag © 1979 by Elisabeth Elliot, A Path through Suffering © 1990 by Elisabeth Elliot www.elisabethelliot.org

3. "Be Still and Know That I Am God" anonymous. Public Domain

4. "I Must Tell Jesus," words by Elizabeth Albright Hoffman, Public Domain

5. "Rest In Me" words and music by Brown Banister, Ellie Bannister and Steve Hindalong. Copyright ©2002 New Spring Never Say Never Songs (Admin. By Brentwood-Benson Music Publishing, Inc., 741 Cool Springs Blvd., Franklin TN 37067) Banistucu Music (Admin. By The Loving Company) Used by permission.

6. "Rock Of My Salvation"; words and music by Teresa Muller; Copyright © 1982 by Maranatha! Music. (Admin. By Music Services) CCCM Music (Marantha! Music [Admin. By Music Services]) Used by permission.

7. Shepherd and Lamb Print, Artist Ruth B. Beck

8. "I Can Only Imagine" words and music by Bart Millard. Copyright © 2001, 2002 Simpleville Music (Admin. By Simpleville Music, Inc.). Used by permission.

9. Integrity Music, "I can only Imagine" copyright @integinc.com. Used by permission.